How to Become a

A Handbook for Getting Started in the IT
Industry

Koso Brown

Contents

Introduction

Have you completed a review form after a dinner at a restaurant? If so, have you ever wondered about the optimization of that data? After analysis, the information gathered will be applied to improve your eating experience. Data analysts use computer tools to examine the raw data and produce actionable insights that can help them make wise business decisions.

"The study of analysis" is a basic historical definition of analytics. A more pertinent and up-to-date explanation would contend that "data analytics" is a crucial instrument for obtaining company insights and offering customized client service. For businesses of all kinds, data analytics—sometimes shortened to "analytics"—has grown in significance. Over time, the field of data analytics has expanded and changed steadily while offering numerous advantages.

Data analysts use data to identify and share meaningful insights by methodically looking for patterns and relationships in the data. However, what is considered data? Everything that you can think of. Quantitative data are often numerical in nature. However, anything that can be interpreted in any way, including words, sounds, or images, can also be categorized as data (qualitative data).

Analytics has been used by businesses since Frederick Winslow Taylor introduced time management practices in the 1800s. Henry Ford's measurement of assembly line speed is another example. Analytics started to get increasing attention in the late 1960s when computers started to be used as decision-supporting tools.

Chapter 1: An Overview of the Development of Data Analytics

Finding out that data has been a vital component of human society from the Ancient and Medieval periods is intriguing.

- The phrase "big data" gained popularity in the middle of the 2000s, and several open-source networks emerged, enabling analysts to organize vast amounts of unstructured data using computer tools.

- Four decades ago, we were gathering data offline. Scholars have gathered proof that analysts have been gathering and examining data from Relational Database Management systems (RDBMS). In 1989, Howard Dresser adopted these conclusions.

- The same is true of John Grant's 1600s explanation of the causes of the Bubonic Plague.

- The mathematicians and architects of that era used sophisticated data analytical techniques to create the Great Pyramid in Egypt.

Knowing the Fundamentals of Data Analytics

The field of data analytics is based on the coordinated use of a variety of qualitative and quantitative methodologies to generate data sets that are useful for understanding market trends, generating insights for businesses, and assisting governments in making choices. Data analytics is now thought to be one of the primary factors igniting or sustaining the digital economy. We utilize some of the most to synthesize substantial amounts of data.

"Rough data" is the first step in the process of becoming an analyst. Without context, raw statistics are jumbled and practically incomprehensible. Only when we have restored order to chaos can we extract knowledge from them that is truly helpful? Thus, the data analytics process includes the steps of gathering, preparing, and arranging data.

Furthermore, a variety of strategies are used in effective data analytics to facilitate the process. Programming, statistics, visualization, and other subjects are among them. Fortunately, many of these methods have been automated to speed up the process. Some are even growing into independent fields. But a competent data analyst will be at least somewhat familiar with them all.

Recognizing the Various Forms of Data Analytics

Now that we are familiar with the fundamentals of data analytics, let's explore the various varieties of data analytics.

1. **Analysis:** Based on his diagnosis, the physician prescribes you a medication. Have you ever wondered what a prescription is like? A prescription is a written recommendation from a physician based on the patient's experience. It is perceived as an attempt to tackle a serious and unexpected health issue. Prescriptive analysis, to put it briefly, is an

advice-based analysis that might prevent a disastrous business decision or avert an unanticipated event.

2. **Predictive Analytics:** As the name suggests, analytics entails the discovery of future events. For example, before releasing a product or service, a soon-to-be start-up may wish to ascertain future market trends.

3. **Diagnostic Analytics:** Examining the what, where, why, and how is part of this. You can mine and evaluate information unique to a location with the use of diagnostic data. It will assist in providing answers to queries like, "Why are there more cancer patients in Japan?"

4. **Descriptive Analytics:** Understanding the pattern is aided when the data analyst provides you with a simple inference of the data. For example, if you need to know how people have used credit cards over the past ten years in terms of behavior. Descriptive

disclosure of the usage trends in the past and present will be part of this.

Why is data analytics important?

The relevance of data analytics can be explained in two easy ways. It helps with decision-making, to start. Second, it is supported by evidence. When these two qualities are combined, data analytics becomes a powerful instrument. It is far more scientific to address problems by basing decisions on empirical data rather than on opinion or "gut feel." Although data analytics is not perfect, it is the most effective tool available for forecasting future patterns and making inferences about historical occurrences.

Additionally, there are numerous social applications for data analytics. Data analytics is frequently promoted online as a tool for business information, such as forecasting future sales or guiding marketing and product development expenditures.

Chapter 2: What is the role of a data analyst?

Now that we are clear on what data analytics are, let's examine what a data analyst's actual responsibilities are.

It is your duty as a data analyst to transform unstructured data into insightful knowledge. You will use data and the insights it offers to solve certain problems or provide answers to particular questions after going through the data analysis process, which we'll go over in the next section.

Afterward, you will use these insights to inform important decision-makers and stakeholders so they can act or make plans appropriately. Simultaneously, data analysts can be in charge of establishing standards for data quality and managing the general procedures for gathering and storing data.

The activities and responsibilities that are usually stated in data analyst job descriptions are a wonderful way to get an idea of what a data analyst works daily. As a data analyst, you can anticipate performing the following tasks based on real job descriptions that were placed on indeed.com:

- While data models, measures, and infrastructure are being established, create and update documentation about them.
- Develop and maintain dashboards
- Build and customize reports
- Visualize and present findings to key stakeholders
- Finding, evaluating, and deciphering patterns and trends in large, intricate data sets
- Sort and purify the data.
- Gather information from primary, secondary, and/or other sources.
- Prioritize company needs and define key performance indicators (KPIs) in close collaboration with management.
- Create and put into use data collection methods and databases.

What is the difference between a data scientist and a data analyst?

It's possible that you've previously read some material discussing data science and conducted some studies on the job of a data analyst. Although these two names are sometimes used synonymously, they refer to two distinct professional pathways with different goals and skill requirements.

Data analysts, as we've already discussed, use an organization's data to interpret it for decision-makers. Through the analysis of data trends and the creation of dashboards and visualizations for wider consumption, their work focuses on providing answers to problems and formulating solutions.

Next, utilizing data mining and machine learning, a data scientist will delve further into the data to find patterns. To support or refute their findings, they will set up experiments and then create models and tests.

After that, they will provide recommendations for future actions a company should take based on their findings.

To put it briefly, data scientists are mostly interested in the future, whereas data analysts focus on the past.

What are data analytics significant?

Data analytics is essential for businesses since it comprises computations and statistical insights derived from natural deductions from people's experiences. Below is a summary of some of the factors contributing to data analytics' increasing significance.

1. Aligned operations: As a marketer, data analytics can help you better understand what your end users are viewing, which will enable you to create campaigns that are more insightful and in line with your customers' needs and thought processes.

2. Smarter Decision Making: By improving your

market recognition, data analytics can help you reduce needless losses and save money. It lets you find more recent target markets. By using data analytics, you can skip the guessing and get right to the point.

3. Enhanced Customer Services: As a company, you can design customized services to meet the demands and specifications of your clients. It may also facilitate the development of an enduring rapport with your client.

4. Adopting an Effective Marketing Strategy: You can achieve the best marketing outcomes by fine-tuning your strategies with the use of data analytics.

Which kinds of data analysts are there?

As you may have been able to infer thus far, data analysis serves a significant purpose with applications in numerous sectors.

But data analytics is far more than just increasing a business's revenue. Additionally, it's applied in medical settings to enhance patient care. It's presently being used in agriculture to change how the world is fed. Governments even utilize it to combat problems like human trafficking. Thus, a career in data analytics can be right for you if you desire to enhance both business and society!

Here are some typical titles you might see on job adverts about data analyst kinds and job titles:

- Intelligence analyst
- Operations analyst
- Market research analyst
- Medical and healthcare analyst
- Business systems analyst
- Business intelligence analyst

Chapter 3: What are the duties and procedures that a data analyst performs?

As a data analyst, it is your responsibility to discover problems and find solutions by completing each phase of the data analytics process. You can decide to focus on a specific field, like data engineering or data visualization, as your career develops. However, as a novice, it's critical to understand the procedure in its entirety.

What then are the main responsibilities and procedures that a data analyst ought to adhere to? While it may not be as simple as just doing one action after another (you might find yourself going back and repeating processes, etc.), the primary tasks are as follows:

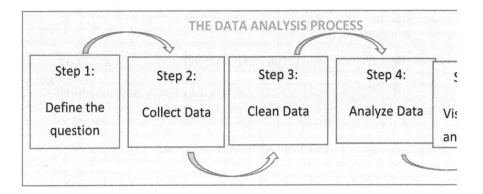

1. Defining a question

The first thing you must do is specify your goal. This is the most difficult step in the process, in some ways. This is because issues may not always start with what appears to be an evident problem.

Let's take an example where you are employed by a corporation that wants to increase sales. Senior management is determined to accomplish this goal by introducing a range of new items. Because of this, you have to invest a lot of time and money in determining which items to develop, which markets to introduce them into, and other factors.

But if you ask some more questions up front, you might find that the company's current products are fine; the issue is with the sales process, which leads to low customer satisfaction and fewer repeat business. With this knowledge, you may discover that spending money on sales training will increase revenue at a significantly reduced expense.

Even though this is only a hypothetical situation, it shows how important it is to investigate a problem from several perspectives before devoting a significant amount of effort to it. It also entails having no problem telling management that their new product idea is incorrect and standing up to authority. Gaining a thorough grasp of the requirements and needs of the company, monitoring KPIs and other measures, and so on are all necessary to define the question you wish to answer. This is normally the time when you do some preliminary analysis as well.

2. Collecting data

Finding the data that will help you answer the question is the next step once you've recognized it. This can be either qualitative or quantitative data (like customer evaluations or marketing stats). To be more precise, there are three types of data: first-party data, which is directly gathered by you or your organization; second-party data, which is another organization's first-party data; and third-party data, which is compiled by a third party from a variety of sources.

You'll need to come up with a plan for gathering these data if you don't already have access to them. Surveys, social media monitoring, website analytics, internet tracking, and other activities might fall under this category. You're ready to clean the data once you have it at your disposal, regardless of how it was collected.

3. Data cleaning

Most recently gathered data will be in an unprocessed format. This indicates that it hasn't been arranged, proofread, or anything else yet. The data must be cleaned to make it ready for analysis. To get it into a more acceptable state, this entails using a range of tools and techniques (including specialized algorithms, generic software, and exploratory investigations).

Errors, duplication, and outliers can be eliminated, unnecessary data can be eliminated (i.e., data that doesn't support your study), the data can be reorganized more effectively, gaps can be filled, and so on. Once this is finished, the data will be verified. This entails making sure it satisfies your needs. You'll frequently discover that it doesn't, in which case you'll have to take a step back.

Data cleansing is therefore regarded as an iterative process. Data wrangling refers to the process of combining data collection and cleanup.

4. Conducting an analysis

You can begin analyzing your dataset as soon as it is organized and clean. There are many different kinds of data analysis, and choosing the one that is most appropriate for the job at hand can be difficult. We'll give a summary of the four primary types of data analytics to keep things easy.

THE FOUR MAIN TYPES OF DATA ANALYSIS

Descriptive	Diagnostic	Predictive
What happened?	Why did it happned ?	What is likely to happen in future

Descriptive analytics comes first. To do this, a dataset's features are summed up (or described) to make it easier to understand. Although it's not typically utilized to reach strong conclusions, it's a helpful starting point for determining how to look into the data more.

21

The next goal of diagnostic analytics is to determine the cause of an event (for example, by looking into correlations between values in a dataset). This aids in problem identification and is frequently applied during the question-defining phase of data analytics.

Lastly, there is prescriptive analytics, which aids in choosing a future course of action, and predictive analysis, which helps detect trends based on historical data. Machine learning techniques are occasionally employed to do the latter.

Chapter 4: Communicating your results

The last stage is to share your findings with the people who originally commissioned the study and the insights you've generated. Usually, this entails putting your data into some sort of visual representation—making charts and graphs, for instance.

Making interactive dashboards, documents, reports, or presentations could potentially be a part of it. Although it's simple to ignore the artistic merit of this phase, doing it well is crucial. In addition to accurately interpreting your results, you also need to communicate them in a way that non-technical staff members who are pressed for time can understand. This is crucial because it guarantees that any decisions made are founded on insightful and well-understood information.

In data analytics, what kinds of tools are used?

1. **KNIME:** It's an open-source, graphically driven data integration platform. Machine learning and data mining are done with KNIME. For some functions, the program isn't technically skilled or scalable enough.

2. **Tableau:** One popular tool for data visualization is Tableau. Although it lacks data pre-processing, it is perfect for making worksheets and dashboards.

3. **Microsoft Power IB:** An additional statistical software package that is used for predictive analytics and data visualization that is comparable to SAS. The program offers the advantages of connectivity and frequent updates, but it also has strict rules.

4. **SAS:** a set of statistical programs that business intelligence analysts employ to do predictive analysis. Although the program is reasonably priced, it is very user-friendly and offers first-rate assistance.

5. Apache Spark: The architecture for data processing used here is used to analyze unstructured data. Apache Spark is a quick and simple framework with a strict user interface.

6. Jupyter Notebook: Creating dormant documents is made possible by this online application. This open-source program allows the user to mix equations, statistics, narrative text, and other elements.

7. R: Similar to Python but with a slightly more complicated syntax is another open-source programming language. R has good Big Data Software integration.

8. Python: Python is a very flexible, open-source programming language that is most popular among data analysts and developers worldwide.

9. Excel: Excel is an excellent spreadsheet program that lets you create computations using particular mathematical formulas. It can also assist in producing a graphical statistics depiction.

What skills does a data analyst need?

Depending on their position, data analysts require different sets of abilities. Understanding the industry, you work in, for example, is crucial. But generally speaking, this is something you can pick up on the job.

However, there are a few fundamental abilities that every beginning data analyst must possess before seizing their first chance. These can be separated into two categories: soft skills, or helpful personality attributes that enable you to complete tasks, and hard skills, or technical aptitudes.

❖ Data analysts' technical proficiency

Hard talents can occasionally have a high learning

curve. But anyone can learn them, with enough discipline. Important hard skills needed by data analysts are:

1. **Basic understanding of machine learning:** Nobody will hold you to a high level of expertise as a novice in machine learning—it's a whole field by itself. That said, many jobs in data analytics are based on the principles of machine learning. The theory—supervised learning as opposed to unsupervised learning, for example—should be familiar to you.

2. **Ability to visualize:** The capacity to visualize data via graphs and charts is a fundamental component of data analytics. This aids in the identification of trends, correlations, and patterns. You should be able to use MS Excel to construct tables and charts, or Python to create plots.

3. **Excel skills:** MS Excel is an essential tool for every data analyst's toolkit since it can be used to automate complicated computations or

convert unprocessed data into a comprehensible format. Make sure you are conversant with its primary analytical features.

4. **knowledge of databases:** You'll need to have some knowledge of analytics engines like Spark and database warehousing software like Hive in addition to programming languages. SQL and other database query languages are also necessary to know

5. **Skills in programming:** Programming knowledge is necessary to develop or improve algorithms that automate data analytics operations (such as parsing or re-structuring big datasets). Popular statistical computing languages in data analytics are R and SAS, as well as scripting languages like Python and MATLAB.

6. **Statistics and math:** You'll have an aptitude for math. You might hold a bachelor's or master's degree in computer science,

statistics, or applied mathematics. Though they can be helpful, credentials aren't always required if you're just starting in the industry. That might be enough if you have strong math abilities, such as in algebra and calculus.

❖ Non-technical skills for data analysts

Although they can be improved with practice, soft skills are usually thought to be more innate. The following require a natural flair on your part:

1. **Ethics:** You'll know the value of data privacy, be conscious of your prejudices, and feel at ease communicating results, even if they are unfavorable or unlikely to bring you recognition. It is crucial to follow a strict code of ethics. Without it, data misuse is simple and can have a negative real-world effect on the people and groups that your work affects.

2. **Innovative approaches to solve problems:** Applying your reflective

perspective to certain data-related situations or problems is the process of problem-solving. You'll define an issue, come up with a plan for fixing it, and methodically complete the essential follow-up tasks. Since these assignments will vary each time, you must have an inventive mentality.

3. **Analytical reasoning:** Critical thinking is the ability to ask questions to gain a deeper understanding of what is presented to you. It is arguably the most significant talent in data analytics. You'll approach projects with a logical and deduction-based approach, be naturally curious, and never take anything at face value.

4. **Communication:** In any profession, but particularly in data analytics, communication is essential. Accurate insight collection should come first, but it's also critical to communicate these to larger audiences in an effective manner. You should be very good at

interacting with people, can explain complicated ideas in simple terms, and feel comfortable making presentations and responding to inquiries from non-technical staff.

Which techniques are employed in data analytics?

Before beginning to comprehend the different kinds of methods employed in Data Analytics, we must first comprehend what is

1. **Quantitative Data:** It is arranged in rows and columns as organized data. The kind of data that is measured is called quantitative data.

2. **Qualitative Data:** Qualitative data is predetermined information that must be

gleaned from assumptions made by the other party. Since qualitative data depends on the feelings of the individual, it is challenging to measure.

The various methods of data analysis consist of

1. **Time Series Analysis:** This methodical approach is employed to comprehend what is #trending over an extended duration. Once more, this is a predictive technique that's frequently used to determine market trends, product/service sales, and stock market movements.

2. **Cluster Analytics:** This approach is utilized to detect the pattern present in the dataset. This analytical method is used to comprehend how a campaign affects a certain target audience.

3. **Cohort Analysis:** By breaking up a group into sub-sects or cohorts, one can better comprehend the behavioral pattern of the group rather than analyzing the vast amount of data. You can analyze the behavioral patterns of people born in a specific year by segmenting a college survey, for example, into cohorts. Analysis of cohorts can be done across time. Colonies' interactions with their peers and surroundings have an impact on their behavioral patterns. Studying customer lifecycles is the ideal use for this dynamic analysis.

4. **Factor Analysis:** Usually, this indicates that big numbers are factored into smaller ones. The art of this method is in revealing a pattern to a large number of people. establishing a robust association, for instance, between monthly household income and monthly entertainment expenditures. This association is really strong.

5. **Monte Carlo Simulation:** This is an approach to producing a probability distribution. Most people regularly use this strategy, especially when attempting to figure out the quickest route to a destination. To get a predictive analysis, it is the perfect forecasting technique.

6. **Regression Analysis:** a variation on analysis that finds the commonalities between several independent and dependent variables. Predictive measures are calculated and taken into account in Regression Analysis.

Chapter 5: Importance of Data Analytics

The majority of departments in businesses today employ data analytics to look at the past and forecast the future. These actions can have several positive effects on an organization. These advantages consist of:

1. Enhanced performance of the business

Gathering and analyzing supply chain data can assist in identifying bottlenecks, manufacturing delays, and potential issues down the road. Data analytics may assist in determining the best supply for each of an organization's products when it comes to inventory levels. This facilitates the identification and prompt resolution of problems for organizations.

2. Boost your ability to make decisions

Businesses can stop financial losses by using data

analytics. If a modification is made, prescriptive analysis would advise how to respond to these changes to optimize profit, whereas predictive analysis would identify the future behaviors of the customers. For example, suppose a business wants to raise the cost of its goods. They may create a model to see how this modification would impact demand from customers. Testing can verify the outcomes of this model. This would shield against bad financial choices.

3. Manage risks

Businesses face a variety of risks, such as employee or customer theft, legal liabilities, and an overabundance of inventory items. Organizations may control and avoid risks with the aid of data analytics. A retail company, for instance, can identify which of its outlets are most likely to experience theft by using a propensity model. This would assist in determining whether to move the store or increase security.

4. Boost security

Companies look at historical security breaches and identify the flaws that resulted in them using data analytics. IT professionals can identify the source and course of security breaches by analyzing, processing, and visualizing audit logs with the use of analytics solutions. By employing analytical models that identify peculiar or aberrant behavioral patterns, they can also thwart future attempts. To detect attempted breaches and warn security experts, these models can be configured with monitoring and alerting systems.

5. Track the performance of the product

Data analytics is used to monitor how customers behave when using goods or services. It can be used to determine a number of things, such as why sales are low, what products customers purchase, why they purchase them, how much they spend on these purchases, and how to improve the way you market your goods. Businesses can make financial decisions, such as establishing a niche to target or adjusting product prices, by analyzing the behavior of their audience.

6. Predict future trends

Data analytics allows organizations to forecast future developments and trends. Organizations may stay at the top of their market by creating future-focused products and services with the help of predictive analysis technologies. By employing effective marketing strategies, these companies may generate demand for their products and increase their market share. They can even secure patents for innovative ideas to keep a competitive edge and increase revenue.

7. Lower the operational expenses

Even though hiring a data analyst can be costly, the

long-term savings outweigh the costs. You can protect your data, avoid financial danger, and take other potentially life-saving actions with competent data analysis. Additionally, companies employ data analytics to identify departments that are overspending and those that require additional funding. This reduces expenses, particularly those associated with operations and production, and eventually, technology takes the place of manual labor.

8. Data Analytics Applications

Data analytics applications have become better over time as a result of developments in the IT industry. Novel and inventive uses for data analytics have been prompted by the emergence of new technological trends such as big data and the Internet of Things (IoT). Among them are:

9. Results of an Internet web search

Analytics are used by search engines such as Google,

Amazon e-commerce search, Bing, and others to organize data and present the most relevant search results. This suggests that the majority of search engine operations make use of data analytics. When storing web data, data analytics collects vast amounts of information provided by various pages and organizes it using keywords. Analytics also aids in the relevance-based ranking of web pages within each group.

Similarly, while presenting search results, each word the user types serves as a keyword. Once more, data analytics is utilized to search a certain collection of web pages and present the one that most closely fits the term intent.

10. Digital advertising and marketing

Data analytics is a tool used by marketers to gain audience insight and increase conversion rates. These two sub-applications each have various tasks that are completed with data analytics. Digital advertising specialists employ analytics to determine the demographics of the target audience, including age, gender, race, and likes and dislikes. They divide their audience into groups based on interests and behavior using this technology as well.

Experts also employ data analytics to spot patterns and create content that is pertinent for sustained engagement to achieve high conversion rates. They achieve this by using analytics trends to examine purchasing patterns and frequency.

11. Security

Data analytics, particularly predictive analytics, is used by security professionals to identify potential criminal or security breach scenarios. They are also able to look into recent or previous attacks. Analyzing how IT systems were compromised during an attack, further conceivable flaws, and end-user or device behavior implicated in a security breach are all made possible by analytics.

Some cities keep an eye on high-crime regions by using data analytics. They keep an eye out for tendencies in crime and use these patterns to forecast potential future crimes. This keeps the city safe without endangering the lives of police personnel.

12. Detecting fraud

Data analytics is used by numerous companies across various industries to identify fraudulent activity. Pharmaceutical, banking, finance, tax, retail, and other industries are among them. Predictive analysis is used to evaluate the accuracy of individual tax returns to detect tax fraud. This kind of analytics is used by the Internal Revenue Service (IRS) to forecast potentially fraudulent activity.

It is also employed in the analysis of communication to detect bank fraud. Data analytics is used by banks to be in continual contact with their clientele. By utilizing data analysis techniques, they can identify fraudulent activity by reviewing past communication data with a certain customer.

13. Education

Data analytics can be used by policymakers to enhance management choices and educational programs. Both administrative administration and educational experiences would be enhanced by these apps.

We can create curricula by gathering preference data from every student to improve the curriculum. This would result in a more effective system where students learn the same material in several ways. Additionally, high-quality student data can support more sensible decisions about sustainable management and resource allocation. Data analytics, for instance, might inform administrators of which resources students utilize less frequently or which subjects pique their interest the least.

Data Analytics' Problems and Solutions

Risk managers need to know a lot about data

analytics. They facilitate better decision-making, raise responsibility, enhance financial stability, and assist staff in tracking performance and predicting losses. Not persuaded? View our two blog postings on the subject, Why Data Analytics Should Be Used by All Risk Managers and Six Reasons Why Data Is Essential to Risk Management.

It's easier said than done, though, to attain these advantages. Risk managers may face several obstacles in their efforts to gather and apply analytics. Thankfully, there is a fix:

1. Data visualization

Data is frequently best presented visually in the form of graphs or charts to be easily understood and effective. Even though these tools are really helpful, creating them by hand is challenging. It is annoying and time-consuming to have to gather data from several sources and enter it into a reporting tool.

Report building is made possible with the push of a mouse by robust data systems. Decision-makers and staff will have easy access to the current information they require in an engaging and instructive manner.

Chapter 5: How much data is being gathered?

With the advent of big data and today's data-driven enterprises, risk managers and other staff members frequently feel overburdened by the volume of data being gathered. Every event and interaction that occurs daily may be reported to an organization, providing analysts with hundreds of interconnected data sets.

A data system that automatically gathers and arranges information is required. In the current context, doing this step by hand is superfluous and takes far too much time. Employees can take action on the data instead of wasting time processing it by using an automated system.

1. Gathering actionable and timely data

It's challenging to sift through the abundance of data and find the insights that are most urgently required.

Overworked staff members might not thoroughly examine data or might just concentrate on the measurements that are simplest to gather rather than those that provide value. It could also be hard for an employee to obtain real-time insights into what is going on if they have to manually sort through data. Decision-making can be seriously harmed by outdated information.

This problem can be resolved with the use of a data system that gathers, arranges, and automatically notifies users of trends. Workers just generate a report with their goals input and the answers to the questions that matter most to them. Decision-makers may be certain that they are making decisions based on accurate and comprehensive information when they have access to real-time reports and warnings.

2. Increasing the size of data analysis

Lastly, when a company grows and the amount of data it collects increases, analytics can be challenging to scale. Information gathering and report creation get more and more complicated. To handle this problem, the organization needs a system that can expand with it.

Even though it could take some time to overcome these obstacles, data analysis has several advantages that make the effort worthwhile. Make immediate improvements to your company and think about purchasing a data analytics system.

The cloud-based Claims, Incident, and Risk Management System from ClearRisk offers countless report possibilities along with automatic data submission. Your start producing impressive analytics will impress management!

3. Budget

Budgeting is another issue that risk managers

frequently deal with. Since risk is frequently a tiny department, getting permission for large acquisitions like an analytics system can be challenging.

Risk managers can obtain funding for data analytics by calculating a system's return on investment and presenting a compelling business case for the advantages it will provide. See our blog post here for additional details on how to win people around to the idea of implementing a risk management software system.

4. Shortage of skills

Talent shortages in some businesses cause problems with analysis. In those without official risk departments, this is particularly valid. Workers might not be equipped with the skills necessary to perform in-depth data analysis.

There are two methods to lessen this challenge: having an analysis system that is simple to use and incorporating analytical competency into the hiring process. While the second approach will make the analytical process easier for all parties, the first approach guarantees that talents are available. Anybody, with any level of ability, can use this kind of technology.

5. Anxiety or confusion

Even though they are aware of the advantages of automation, users may experience anxiety or confusion when transferring from conventional data processing techniques. Nobody enjoys change, particularly if it disturbs their comfort zone or usual routine.

It's critical to demonstrate how adjustments to analytics will streamline the position and make it more purposeful and satisfying to solve this HR issue. Employees can spend more time acting on insights by doing away with pointless processes like data collection and report construction when they have access to complete data analytics.

6. Data of poor quality

Nothing is more detrimental to data analytics than data that is not accurate. Reliability is compromised in output if input is subpar. Human error during data entry is a major contributor to erroneous data. If the analysis is applied to decision-making, this could have serious adverse effects. Asymmetrical data is another problem, where information in one system is out of date because it does not reflect changes made in another system.

These problems are eliminated with a centralized system. With obligatory or drop-down fields, data entry can be done automatically, reducing the possibility of human error. System integrations make sure that modifications made in one place are immediately reflected everywhere.

7. Data from multiple sources

Trying to assess data from several, disparate sources is the next problem. distinct systems frequently contain distinct types of data. Workers might not always be aware of this, which could result in erroneous or inadequate analysis. Combining data by hand takes effort and may restrict insights into what is visible.

An all-inclusive, centralized system will provide staff with access to all kinds of data in one place. This not only reduces the time spent navigating between sources, but it also enables cross-comparisons and guarantees the completeness of data

8. Pressure from the top

As risk management gains traction in businesses, CFOs, and other executives are expecting greater output from risk managers. They anticipate receiving a lot of reports on various types of data and larger returns.

Risk managers may quickly give any requested study and go above and above with a comprehensive analysis system. Additionally, they'll have more time to implement new ideas and increase the department's worth to the company.

Conclusion

One of the most popular fields for investment and study nowadays is data analytics. According to Gartner, by 2025, artificial intelligence and context-driven analytics will displace current technologies. The emergence of data fabrics, data sharing, and connected governance are some of the other important themes that Gartner predicts.

Companies must be well informed about data analytics, including its types and applications, to fully utilize the power of these technologies. Even in a difficult market, corporate success can be driven and results may be accelerated with good analytics implementation.